December 2000

Mum

I hope this brings back good memories
and proves that the best is yet to
come. Can't wait to have you back.

All my love

Amanda

The
Cayman
Islands

The
Cayman
Islands
Island Portrait

J ENNY D RIVER

CARIBBEAN

Dedicated to Stephen and Joshua

First published 2000 by
MACMILLAN EDUCATION LTD
London and Oxford
Companies and representatives throughout the world

ISBN 0–333–76040–9

10	9	8	7	6	5	4	3	2	1
09	08	07	06	05	04	03	02	01	00

Printed in Hong Kong

A catalogue record for this book is available from the
British Library.

All photographs are by the author unless otherwise stated.

Cover photos: beach, Bodden Town (front), pink house (back).

Contents

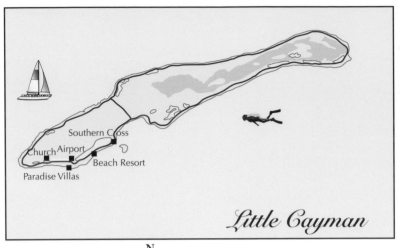

Little Cayman

- Southern Cross
- Church
- Airport
- Beach Resort
- Paradise Villas

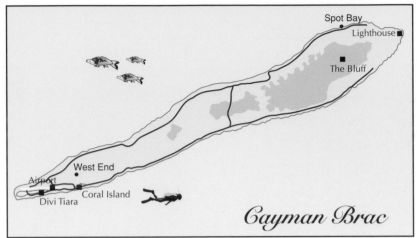

Cayman Brac

- Spot Bay
- Lighthouse
- The Bluff
- West End
- Airport
- Divi Tiara
- Coral Island

81°W — 80°W

Little Cayman — *Cayman Brac*

19°30'N —

Grand Cayman

| 0 | 10 15 miles |
| 0 | 24 Km |

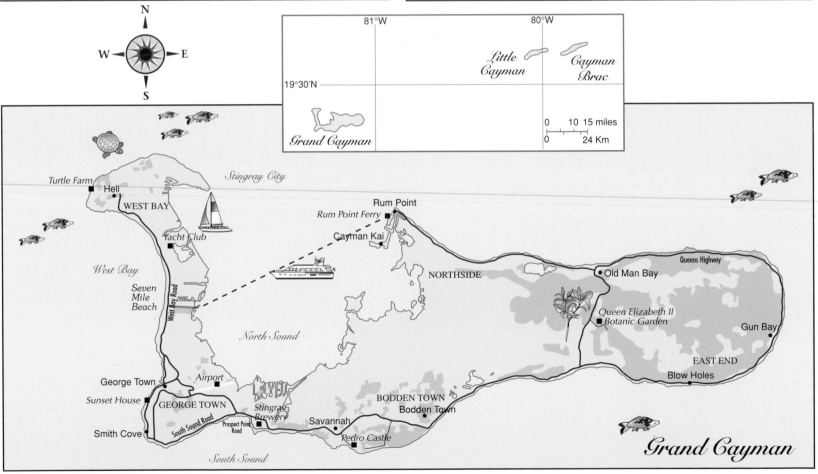

Grand Cayman

- Turtle Farm
- Hell
- **WEST BAY**
- Stingray City
- Rum Point
- *Rum Point Ferry*
- Cayman Kai
- *Yacht Club*
- *West Bay*
- *Seven Mile Beach*
- *West Bay Road*
- *North Sound*
- **NORTHSIDE**
- Old Man Bay
- Queens Highway
- *Queen Elizabeth II Botanic Garden*
- Gun Bay
- George Town
- *Airport*
- *Sunset House*
- **GEORGE TOWN**
- *Stingray Brewery*
- *South Sound Road*
- *Prospect Point Road*
- Smith Cove
- Savannah
- *Pedro Castle*
- **BODDEN TOWN**
- Bodden Town
- **EAST END**
- Blow Holes
- *South Sound*

N · S · E · W

The Cayman Islands

The Cayman Islands are three islands – Grand Cayman, Cayman Brac, Little Cayman – just 480 miles south of Miami, and 189 miles north-west of Jamaica in the Western Caribbean. They total in area 100 square miles. Grand Cayman, the largest, is 76 square miles, Cayman Brac, the second largest, is 14 square miles and Little Cayman is 10 square miles. Grand Cayman is the capital island and is about 80 miles southwest of Little Cayman and about 85 miles southwest of Cayman Brac. Cayman Brac is the most easterly of the three islands, about 5 miles east of Little Cayman. Grand Cayman and Little Cayman are flat, the highest parts are 60 feet above sea level. Cayman Brac has a central limestone ridge, The Bluff, reaching 140 feet at its eastern end. Central areas have luxuriant vegetation in mangrove swamps, a haven for bird and marine life. The population is 34 000 on Grand Cayman, with 2 000 on Cayman Brac and only about 100 on Little Cayman.

History
The islands were first sighted by Columbus in May 1503. He named them 'Las Tortugas' after the turtles he saw swimming in the waters. At that time there was no human life on the Islands. The early inhabitants were a mixture of shipwrecked sailors, buccaneers, army deserters and other adventurers, later joined by slaves brought from Africa. British possession of the Islands was recognised by Spain in the Treaty of Madrid in 1670, and today they remain one of the few British Overseas Territories in the Caribbean.

Climate
Summer or winter, the temperatures in Cayman seldom fall outside the range 65° F (18° C) to 90° F (32° C). The average sea temperature during the winter is 75° F (24° C) and in summer it is 85° F (30° C). High season for tourism is mid-December to mid-April but the flow of visitors now continues year round. Rainfall averages around 60 inches a year. May to October is likely to bring the most rain, but the sun fails to shine on only about six days a year.

Preface

I first went to Grand Cayman working on a commercial for 'Free the Spirit' Impulse Body Spray back in February 1992. I was doing the 'wardrobe' in my days as a fashion stylist. The model – Selina Giles – and I loved the island so much we stayed on for five days after the shoot. In May of that year I was back and stayed in Old Man Bay, Northside for two months. Between then and now I have been back six times.

There are five main areas – George Town, West Bay, Bodden Town, Northside and East End. The book begins in the capital, George Town, drives out along the West Bay Road to West Bay, the Turtle Farm and Hell, back through George Town and out along the South Sound Road past Cathy Church's underwater paradise at Sunset House to Pedro Castle and Bodden Town. We then see the Queen Elizabeth II Botanic Garden in Northside and through Old Man Bay, and to Rum Point (which you can reach direct from the Hyatt on the West Bay Road by means of the Rum Point ferry). Then we drive back to Old Man Bay and out on the Queens Highway past the Tortuga Club through Gun Bay to East End and the Blow Holes.

After this there are a selection of pictures from Cayman Brac and Little Cayman. We stayed at the Divi Tiara on Cayman Brac where you walk straight from your hotel room terrace onto the white sandy beach. On Little Cayman we stayed at Paradise Villas from where you can also walk straight onto the beach, looking out for the iguanas, especially Hungry who is five feet long.

When I was there in April 1998 the National Gallery of the Cayman Islands opened with a stunning exhibition of sculpture. The cultural life of the islands is very rich with the indigenous talent such as Wray Banker and his Native Sons group, Miguel Powery, Horacio Esteban, Al Ebanks, Nasaria Suckoo, Bendel Hydes, Anthony Ramoon, Gladwyn Bush a.k.a. Miss Lassie, and Danny Owens – architect. John Broad, Debbie Chase van der Bol – of Pure Art, Jan Barwick, Margaret Barwick, Charles Long, Joanne Sibley and Lesley Bigelman represent the 'settlers' talent.

Cayman is everything one thinks of as a Paradise Island. It has the most clear and stunningly turquoise waters I have experienced in the Caribbean. The crystalline waters show off the sea life to best advantage. This is why it is in the top three diving sites of the world alongside the Barrier Reef, Australia and the Red Sea, Middle East. Above the water the landscape is completely flat and open – if you are looking for rainforest and mountains this is not your place. Below the water you can dive 'the Wall' and discover that the part above sea level is merely the top of a fantastic mountain of hidden treasure. It has the most exciting pirate tales – you can take a trip on the Jolly Roger and the Valhalla and experience sailing on true tall ships, visit the pirate caves (and graves) at Bodden Town, hear word of mouth stories of the pirate days from older locals, or join in the celebration of the island's pirate history at Pirates Week in October.

Cayman is a truly magic place for me, I love its space and light and incredible sea. I hope this book serves as a memento of an island you know and love well, a guide to those of you lucky enough to be on a visit, or an inducement to book a flight and spend some time there.

Jenny Driver

Jenny Driver, LONDON

Introduction:
A Snapshot of the Cayman Islands

Over the next few pages you will find a thumbnail sketch of the Cayman Islands, for the saga of over 250 years of history cannot ever be fully told, let alone in so brief a space. And a saga it is – from the Islands' history as a haven for buccaneers and pirates; to the Islanders' epic voyages on hand-hewn sailing vessels in pursuit of the green turtle; to their remarkable service in both World Wars; to their equally remarkable reputation as seamen fulfilling the demands of modern merchant shipping; to the Islands' sometimes controversial role as favourite tourist destination and tax haven for companies.

Unless you look specifically for them, it is easy to miss the Cayman Islands the first time you scan a map of the Caribbean. And even if you look for them, they may not be shown on the first map you happen to pick up. But do take a closer look, and on a large-scale map. At about 19 degrees north, 80 degrees west, imagine an intersection of lines, one traced to the south, and slightly east, of Miami, and one due north-west of Jamaica, and there you will find three tiny coral islands, totalling a mere 100 square miles altogether – the Cayman Islands: Grand Cayman, Little Cayman and Cayman Brac.

The Islands lie along a west-south-west/east-north-east geological faultline which rises to form the peaks of the Sierra Maestra in south-east Cuba. They are the three coralline tips of an underwater ridge, each flanked by deep ocean (down to more than 20 000 feet in the Cayman Trench), with 74 miles of 'the blue' between Grand Cayman and Little Cayman, and 5 miles between Little Cayman and Cayman Brac.

All three Islands have areas of lush green mangrove swamp, patches of often rocky dry woodland, and coasts lined with glittering white sand beaches, ironshore (jagged, lichen-blackened masses of coral), and loose coral rocks. Grand Cayman and Little Cayman have similar proportions of swamp, beach and reef. Their fringing reefs run virtually parallel to the shore, along the relatively shallow shelf between shore and the sheer deep-water Cayman Wall of scuba fame. The reefs form a protective barrier against the surge of the open sea, and are especially important in protecting the very shallow lagoons known locally as Sounds.

But there are differences too, on Little Cayman and the Brac woodland is sparser and terrain is rockier than on the larger island. In fact the Brac is dominated by its ancient limestone Bluff, a monolithic outcrop which rises to 140 feet at Spot Bay, the eastern-most and highest point of the Islands. It was in the caves along its sides that many Brackers found shelter from the devastating hurricane of 1932; and it is the Bluff which locally is taken to symbolise the Brackers' proverbial hardiness.

The waters around the Islands are exceptionally clear. Within them can be viewed the teeming, colourful swirl of reef life: many species of corals, reef fish, sponges, rays, bivalves and crustaceans. Sharks, which are not plentiful here, will generally only be seen outside the reef, likewise the more frequent passing schools of large game fish. Closer to shore, around the red mangrove roots of Grand Cayman's North Sound or Little Cayman's South Hole Sound, you can observe the fecund breeding ground of this rich habitat, and discover just how and why the murky swamps are vital to Cayman's status as a scuba paradise.

The physical environment of Cayman has always been a significant economic resource. In the days of armed contest between European powers bent on conquest in the West Indies, their privateers and buccaneers, as well as ordinary sailors, often staved off disease with fresh turtle meat and fresh water obtained from the Cayman Islands. In the eighteenth century the settlers made their living from local plants, including ironwood and the endemic Silver Thatch Palm, but they also exported plant products such as mahogany and cotton to Jamaica. Meanwhile they applied and developed their skills in building boats, ranging further and further across the western Caribbean to Central and South America and the east coast of the USA, becoming adept seamen and probably the best turtle fishermen in the world.

Now ease of access by air and sea, clear water and healthy reefs, sunny hot weather and beautiful beaches, the presence of rare species of flora and fauna – Ghost Orchids and Blue Iguanas – all make the Islands attractive to visitors and expatriate residents alike. The modern transformation of Cayman came about partly because of increased efficiency in transport and communication. When brigs and caravels plied the Caribbean in the seventeenth and eighteenth centuries, Cayman, being small and out of the way, was not easy to find. The steamships of the nineteenth century kept the islands off the map, because they were not in the most direct shipping lanes.

The effect of this prolonged relative isolation was the development of indigenous forms of social organisation and political rule. A sort of home-grown democracy and a sense of both territorial and personal independence were established, both of which continue even now to buttress the Islands' resolute individuality in forging their own path forward.

Cayman was formally associated with Jamaica for much of its history. Yet the connection was not in fact a close one, consisting chiefly of a few trade links and the supply of some professional services (for example doctors and magistrates). For a time, Cuba provided similar resources. But the strongest orientation ran to the north, especially from the late nineteenth century – to Britain for historical and constitutional reasons, and to the USA because of its location, the turtle trade, and the job opportunities it afforded, both on land and at sea. Most of this trade and travel took place using Cayman-built vessels, which began to be motorised in the 1950s around the same time that the first airstrip opened. The first cars had arrived in the 1930s and local roads were then improved. So poor had the roads been previously that most movement between districts depended on the small boats known as the cat-boat and the dory. On land, most people walked the narrow footpaths; a few used horses or mules.

It is commonly said that the modern transformation of Cayman started in the 1960s with legislation to encourage offshore financial business. It was also at this time that telephones became available on a fairly wide scale, and a regular aeroplane service began. But it can be argued that the process began even earlier, with the postwar shift from a subsistence and barter based economy to a modern cash economy. This was marked by the increasing employment, on cash contracts, of highly prized Caymanian seamen aboard the ships of National Bulk Carriers of the USA.

Whatever its origins, the Cayman Islands and Grand Cayman in particular, have enjoyed a virtually unbroken economic boom since the early 1970s, generating a level of public revenues and private incomes to make possible a network of paved roads, a glut of motor vehicles, and widespread access to electronic media – telephone, fax, Internet, e-mail, three local radio stations and one TV (Cable) company, as well as a daily local newspaper and a wide selection of international newspapers, magazines, movies, videos, and recorded music.

This economic buoyancy was not planned in the strictest sense, but it has been vigorously promoted and sufficiently regulated to avoid some of the worst excesses of rapid growth. Tourism and the tax-haven business are generally seen as the motors of the local economy – providing direct public revenues through fees, as well as creating demand for labour, support services, and supplies of goods and materials. So in tourism, personnel are needed to service accommodation, as well as to provide staff for popular water-sports such as scuba, snorkelling, fishing, sailing, kayaking, submarine rides, and so on. Similarly the banks and trust companies, legal and accountancy firms and company management concerns, all require skilled staff to provide services to local and offshore clientele. By the mid-1990s over a million tourists were visiting annually, and Cayman had arrived as one of the top financial centres in the world.

The rapid increase in demand for labour quickly overtook what could be supplied by the small and slow-growing population, even when the bulk of the Brac labour force migrated to Grand Cayman where the growth was concentrated. Most of the additional labour came from the UK, Canada, and the USA in the north; from Jamaica, Trinidad, and elsewhere in the West Indies; from Nicaragua, Honduras, Brazil and elsewhere in Latin America; from China, India, the Philippines and elsewhere in the east.

It has been the primary aim of public policy in this period to spur growth, through direct marketing and legislation facilitating speed and ease of operations, an honest and efficient bureaucracy, reliable utilities, electronic communications and so on. By the late 1990s the pace of growth was being called into question, because of apparent and prospective impacts both on the physical environment and on the sense of social well-being and cultural integrity of the people of the Islands.

To compete effectively, the people of Cayman have had to work hard and maintain high standards. Caymanians are often described as a peaceful and friendly people because it is common for visitors to encounter an unaffected warmth and gentleness in daily dealings with them. In this context it may be mentioned that the Christian church (from Catholic to fundamentalist, including some whose services are conducted in Spanish) retains the only centres of public worship, though there is now a small Ba'hai community, along with small numbers of Muslims, Hindus and Buddhists. Up to the late 1990s these were not known to hold public worship locally. The presence of such worshippers together with the teaching of the basics of their beliefs in schools and exposure of the increasing numbers of students obtaining tertiary training overseas, could produce a change in this profile in future. This is one rather paradoxical result of the secularisation of education, which was originally the charge of the churches. The Government now takes responsibility for a network of primary schools, a middle and a secondary school, though the United Church continues to operate its own school, as do the Catholics, Wesleyans, Baptists, two Churches of God, and the Seventh Day Adventists. All work towards either the CXC, British GCSEs and A Levels, or matriculation at the American high school level. In addition, the Community College of the Cayman Islands, also government grant-aided, offers A Levels, technical training for subjects from banking to cookery, accredited Associate degrees, and (through the University of the West Indies) distance-learning programmes. The Cayman Islands Law School issues law degrees by arrangement with the University of Liverpool. The American-style International College of the Cayman Islands offers undergraduate and postgraduate degrees validated by one of the regional boards of accreditation in the USA. Every year, dozens of high school graduates continue through to tertiary education, many of them overseas. The Islanders enjoy a high standard of health, partly due to the easy availability and high take-up rate of immunisations against communicable diseases; partly also due to effective control programmes against disease vectors such as mosquitoes. The focus of the publicly subsidised healthcare system remains on secondary-care treatment, hence the high degree of investment in plant, equipment and staff for a new hospital. Private practitioners, of which there are many, have a similar focus. To some degree the need to promote a healthy lifestyle in order to curb the 'lifestyle diseases' now chiefly accounting for deaths on the Islands, is being answered privately – through exercise gyms, dance and martial arts clubs, and the programmes of a large and active sporting community.

Entertainment and cultural activity also contribute to a healthy lifestyle, whether one watches or stages a theatrical or dance production, enjoys live comedy, music and dancing – with or without alcohol – visits a museum or gallery exhibition, or participates in workshops centred on painting, writing plays or poetry, modelling clay or carving wood; there are many such opportunities as bodies like the National Museum, the Cultural Foundation, the National Gallery, Dance Unlimited, and the National Trust, develop their outreach in a community becoming ever more conscious of its need to understand and express its place in the world.

Photography is the medium that Jenny Driver has chosen for expressing her understanding of the Cayman Islands' sense of itself. She has provided the pictures – unstaged and telling pictures – of our unique places and people. It is up to you to finish the journey of discovery that Jenny Driver's camera has begun for you. This book does not pretend to show you all of the Cayman Islands. But it shows enough to intrigue, to make you want to see more for yourself.

So, as we say in the Islands, 'Go head'n'look, nuh!'

GRAND CAYMAN

Aerial photo of George Town   Photo: Ed Powers

The Governor's Residence   Photo: Ed Powers

Policemen on the Queen's Birthday
Photo: Ed Powers

The Cayman National Bank Building

Sir Vassell Johnson, the original Financial Secretary of the Cayman Islands Government

Ansbacher House, George Town

The W.S. Walker Building – one of George Town's first Law Firms

View from George Town Harbour

Statue of James M. Bodden opposite the Law Courts, George Town

The National Museum at George Town Harbour

Whitehall Bay

14

Cruise ship at George Town

Fisherman in front of the Tower Building and Wholesome Bakery, George Town

Fishermen, George Town Harbour

Shells for sale, George Town

Fisherman, George Town Harbour

'Igor', tender for the deep-diving submarine, the submarine 'Atlantis', and the sub-shuttle, George Town Harbour

John Doak, architect, in front of George Town Harbour

Alia Solomon on the beach

The Public Beach, West Bay Road

Cruise ship at sunset

The world-renowned author, Dick Francis, on Seven Mile Beach

By the jet-skis, Seven Mile Beach

Just before sunset, Seven Mile Beach

Volley ball on the Public Beach, West Bay Road

Girl on the Public Beach

Playing in the sea

The Yacht Club

Mikey High on the Red Baron on the way to Stingray City

On the Red Baron near Stingray City

Stingray City

The Yacht Club bar at 4.00 pm

The International Fishing Tournament which takes place for eight days in April/May each year

House in West Bay

West Bay

The beach on the way to West Bay

Turtle Farm, West Bay

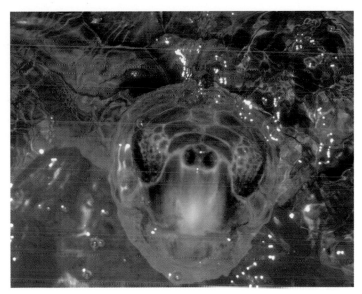

Gary Ebanks at Hell

Policeman

Crosby Ebanks

At Batabano Carnival, Elizabethan Square, George Town

Batabano Carnival

Cathy Church teaching underwater photography

Driftwood signs at Sunset House

54

Banded butterfly fish   Photo: Cathy Church

Grunts   Photo: David Dunbar

Peacock flounder

Anemone *Condylactis gigantea*

Photos: Andrew Sutton

Fan worms

Yellowtail snapper

Gladwyn Bush MBE – 'Miss Lassie'. Visionary painter at her home

Window at Miss Lassie's house

House on the Prospect Point Road

House on the South Sound Road

At Smith Cove

Horacio Esteban

One of his carvings

Debbie Chase van der Bol of Pure Art at the Art Gallery on
South Church Street

Papie Conolly at his Stingray Brewery

Savannah Primary School – in assembly

The Old School House, Savannah

On the road from Savannah to Bodden Town

Man in hammock just past Savannah

The 'Cliff' near Pedro Castle

Pirate on the Jolly Roger

The Jolly Roger

Girl with conch shell on the Jolly Roger

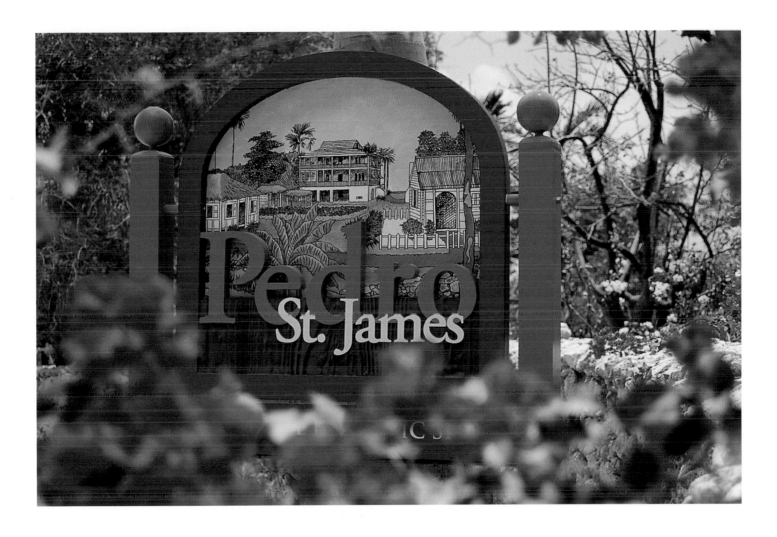

Pedro Castle

Pedro Castle

At Pedro Castle

Pirate graves at Bodden Town

Charles Long in his studio by Pedro Castle

House at Bodden Town

The beach, Bodden Town

Bromeliad 'Burning bush'
Aechmea ramosa x *fulgens* cv. *Burning bush*

Periwinkle *Catharanthus roseus*
Caladium *Caladium bicolour*

The Botanic Park

House in the Heritage Garden at the Queen Elizabeth II Botanic Park

86

Croton *Codiaeum variegatum*

Heliconia *Heliconia caribaea*

Calico flower *Aristolochia grandiflora*

Caladium *Caladium bicolor*

The Botanic Park

Ripening mangos

Ironshore on the beach

Rum Point

On the dock at Rum Point where the 'Rum Pointer' Ferry arrives from the Hyatt, George Town

House at Cayman Kai

Church at Gun Bay

Palms at East End

Blow Holes, East End

Tamika and sea fan, Blow Holes, East End

Deck at East End

CAYMAN
BRAC

The lighthouse

The Bluff

The Texaco garage in Town

Pink House

The Divi Tiara Beach

Tree on the beach at the Divi Tiara

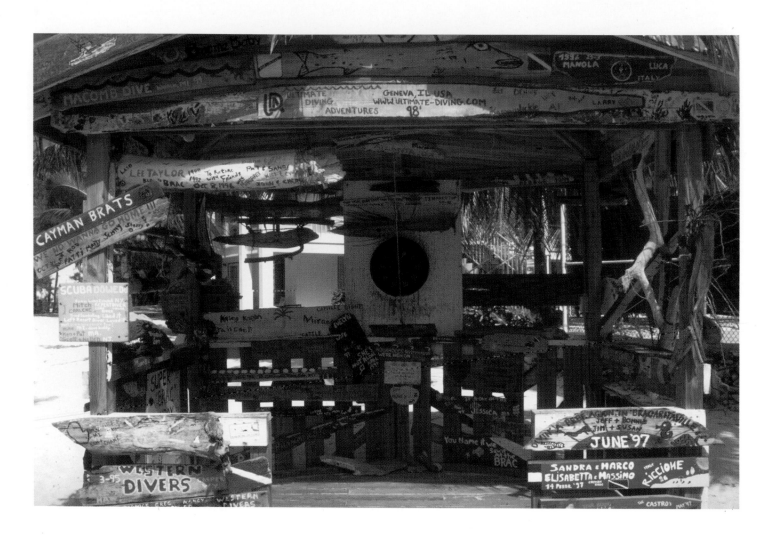

Painted driftwood hut and dart board at the Divi Tiara

Caves

Church

Ginger Cows

Spot Bay Primary School

114

Basketball at the High School

Road

Hammock House

116

LITTLE CAYMAN

Beach at Paradise Villas

Cycling near the airport

Reception of Paradise Villas and the airport

The Church

122

The pool at Paradise Villas

Little Cayman Beach Resort

124

J.A. Ryan, property developer

Southern Cross Dock

Southern Cross

Iguana sign by the airport

Acknowledgements

Nicky Connolly at the Cayman Department of Tourism, Janet Gates at the Cayman Brac Department of Tourism, Andrew Guthrie at the Queen Elizabeth II Botanic Garden, Island Air, British Airways, Jonathan at McCluskey and Assocs, the Divi Tiara Resort on Cayman Brac, Paradise Villas on Little Cayman, Helen Calder and the Sleep Inn on Grand Cayman, Ursula Glatzeder at Dollar Rent a Car, Gladys at Pirates Point, McLauglin Car Rentals on Little Cayman, Nicky & Bunny Watson & family, Mikey High - especially for that idyllic trip to Stingray City on his boat the Red Baron, as always Nick Gillard and Michael Bourne at Macmillan, Barbara Levey and Ed Powers at the Book Nook, Billy Adam at Hobbies & Books, Dwight & Hank Barnes, Cornell Ivon Ebanks, Olivine, Eugene, Belinda, Tamika, Tashanta, Ali & Alia Solomon for their wonderful company and hospitality, Cathy Church, Dave Dunbar at Fish Eye, Aileen Kane at Little Cayman Beach Resort, Rachel Collingwood and Andrew Sutton, John Godfrey at the Hydroponic Farm, Papie Connolly at Stingray Brewery, Miguel Powery, Al Ebanks, Wray Banker, Horacio Esteban, Nasaria Suckoo, Leonard Dilbert & family, Savannah Primary School, Spot Bay Primary School, the John Gray High School, Joanne Sibley, Judson McCoy, Norma Ebanks, Teddy Ebanks, Carmen & Ward Powell, Danny Owens, John Broad, Mark Frazier, Eliza Strachan, Charles Long, Atley Ebanks, Frank McField, Dick Christiansen, John Doak, Anita Ebanks, Catherine Briggs, Rebecca Davidson at Rapid Photo, Crosby Ebanks, Wally Warren - the sculptor from Maine, Geddes Grant at the G & M Diner on Cayman Brac, Lovesa Welds-Hedberg at the Cayman National Bank, Stephen Hall-Jones, Bruce Campbell for his insight into the financial history of Cayman, Sir Vassel Johnson, Gladwyn Bush, Lesley Bigelman, Margaret Barwick, Jan Barwick, Dick Francis, Debbie Chase van der Bol.

Iguana outside the Hungry Iguana Restaurant

130